KW-322-693

Pelham Pictorial Sports Instruction Series

Cliff Temple and Peter Tatlow

GYMNASTICS FOR GIRLS

Pelham Books

First published in Great Britain by
PELHAM BOOKS LTD
52 Bedford Square,
London WC1B 3EF
1977

© Cliff Temple and Peter Tatlow, 1977

All rights reserved. No part of this publication may be reproduced, stored in a retrieval system, or transmitted, in any form or by any means, electronic, mechanical, photocopying, recording or otherwise, without the prior permission of the Copyright owners.

ISBN 0 7207 1013 8

Filmset and printed in Great Britain by
BAS Printers Limited, Over Wallop, Hampshire

An Leabharlann
A
796.4'1
Leitir Ceanainn
Ceard Choláiste Réigiún

GYMNASTICS FOR GIRLS

Also in the Pelham Pictorial Sports Instruction Series

Chester Barnes: Table Tennis
Henry Cooper: Boxing
John Dawes: Rugby Union
Bob Wilson: Soccer
Richard Hawkey: Squash Rackets
Rachael Heyhoe Flint: Women's Hockey
Barry Richards: Cricket
Ken Adwick: Golf
Paul and Sue Whetnall: Badminton
Jack Karnehm: Understanding Billiards and Snooker
Denis Watts: Athletics—Jumping and Vaulting
Howard and Rosemary Payne: Athletics—Throwing
Celia Brackenridge: Women's Lacrosse
Brian Jacks: Judo
W. G. Scull: Gliding and Soaring
John Le Masurier and Denis Watts: Athletics—Track Events
Peter Williams: Canoeing
David Haller: Swimming

Contents

Acknowledgements

Photographic sequences—Mark Shearman.
Technical advice—Mrs Meg Warren, National Women's Senior Squad Coach. Mr W. R. McLoughlin, National Women's Senior Squad Coach and Senior Lecturer in Physical Education at St Mary's College, Twickenham.
Gymnasium facilities—St Mary's College, Twickenham.

Gymnasts
Avril Lennox, Susan Cheesebrough, Elaine Willett, Karen Forbes, Catherine Brookes.

Introduction

In the space of just a few years, gymnastics has changed from being a minor to a major sport. Ever since a tiny seventeen-year-old Russian girl named Olga Korbut caught the imagination of the world through her performances and personality at the 1972 Munich Olympic Games, millions of girls all over the world have wanted to emulate such grace and artistry.

Some gymnastics experts feel that Olga's contribution to the 'boom' has been exaggerated, with other even more talented gymnasts being over-shadowed by the spotlight on the elfin Russian. But that is to ignore the fact that there have been great gymnasts for a long time. Somehow, though, they did not project the charisma of Olga, and that is what caught the public attention. Then, and only then, were the many millions of television viewers alerted to the other outstanding exponents of the sport. So gymnastics as a whole owes a great debt to Olga Korbut, whose individual popularity even led to a fan club being formed for her in Los Angeles.

The subsequent boom in gymnastics, particularly noticeable in Britain where gymnastics clubs were practically bursting at the seams and crying out for more coaches and facilities, was given another huge push at the 1976 Montreal Olympic Games, where an even younger girl, fourteen-year-old Nadia Comaneci of Rumania, became one of the stars of the whole Games.

With her immaculate performances, scoring an unheard-of total of seven 'perfect' 10.0 marks during the competition, gymnastics had found another queen. Olga was not forgotten, but this time she had to share the spotlight.

Today British gymnastics is still growing, as thousands of budding young Olgas and Nadias form the base of a giant pyramid which is essential if Britain is to produce its own world-beating stars in the future.

Why are so many attracted to the sport? Perhaps because in gymnastics they find the most acceptable sport, socially speaking. Although girls are taking part in more and more sporting activities, there are still a few people who consider sport of any kind to be an 'unladylike' pursuit. They are diminishing

CCCP

1 (Left) *Olga Korbut, the girl who started the gymnastics boom with her performances at the 1972 Munich Olympics.*

2 *Nadia Comaneci of Rumania: an Olympic gold medallist at the age of fourteen.*

in number, of course, as convincing evidence dismisses this view. The vast benefits to your health obtained from sport make it not only an acceptable but a positively desirable hobby. And of all the sports open to girls, gymnastics, with its close parallels in ballet and its strong artistic overtones, has a particular lure.

Also, the knowledge that a fourteen-year-old girl can become an Olympic champion is probably a great boost to young people who so often are impatient for success. But it must be remembered that Nadia Comaneci started gymnastics at seven years of age, having already shown a natural aptitude, and then worked very, very hard in the years leading up to Montreal.

One thing which must never be overlooked is that just because there are so many more youngsters taking part now in gymnastics, and more coaches and clubs available, success is no easier to achieve. It is as hard as it always was; harder, in fact, because there are so many more rivals. However, as with most things, there is a large element of satisfaction to be gained through doing something well, even if you never win a gold medal. The conquering of yourself, by learning to execute and perfect something you could only think about when you started, is in itself a worthwhile target.

This book cannot coach you to an Olympic gold medal. It is not, in fact, a coaching book but what it *can* do is to show you the sort of things on the four pieces of Olympic apparatus—floor, vault, beam and bars—which every gymnast, including Olga Korbut and Nadia Comaneci, had to learn before they moved on to more difficult elements. There is an old Chinese proverb which says that 'Every long journey begins with just a single step'. Reading this book could be your first step, but to continue along the path you must actually learn to do the exercises shown here, and for that you will need to go along to a gymnastics club. Find out if your school gymnasium is used by a club in the evenings or at weekends, or write to the British Amateur Gymnastics Association at 23A, High Street, Slough, Berks, SL1 1DY, to discover where your nearest club is situated.

A beginning

Before you even begin to think about your first competitive exercise, you will need a grounding and basic conditioning programme in order to get you used to the different requirements of each piece of apparatus. The club coach will help you here, but there are a certain number of basic principles which you must remember throughout your gymnastics career.

The first is always to warm up thoroughly before training or competition. The muscles cannot work efficiently when cold, and to try to force them to do so will often result in injury. Instead, start with some gentle stretching exercises, becoming more vigorous as your body begins to respond and, literally, to 'warm up'. Often clubs will organize a mass warm-up before a training session, but there will come a day when you have to do it on your own, particularly at a competition when your coach cannot be with you permanently.

You will have to time your warm-up

properly before a competition, and once under way you must keep warm until it is your turn on the apparatus. There is no point in warming up an hour before you are due on, and then sitting down for half an hour to watch others. You will simply get cold again, and your warm-up will be wasted. It is a very good idea to have a tracksuit, or old jumper and trousers, to wear over your leotard when not actually competing, to keep yourself as warm as possible, for when your muscles are finely tuned you must look after them.

Good posture is vital for any gymnast, and this should come with work in the gym, but one thing on which you can work from the very start is a neat and tidy appearance. So often a little attention to detail (or lack of it) can enhance or ruin a gymnastic performance, however good.

If you have long hair, tie it back (Olga-type bunches are very popular among gymnasts); fringes over the eyes give the effect that your head is down. And, of course, long hair flying wildly around in some exercises not only looks untidy but could actually impede your vision and judgement.

Your leotard should be neither too baggy nor too tight, and you should not be wearing any jewellery or other distractions. If you *feel* smart as you approach an exercise it will add something to your performance. Remember that the judges' first impression of you comes when you walk on to the floor, and although they will not take off marks for untidy appearance, if they see you slouch on with carelessly attended hair, giggling, and pulling faces at your friends in the audience, they will not be very impressed. And never, ever chew gum!

So having established the essential disciplines of a gymnast, and bearing in mind that only constant and dedicated training are the keynotes, we are ready to look more closely at each of the four components of Olympic gymnastics.

CHAPTER ONE

Floorwork

The first thing you will notice about the floor exercise is that although it is one of the four pieces of Olympic apparatus, it is unlike the others because there are no actual objects involved. You will simply be moving around on mats in a twelve-metre square without help or hindrance from a horse, bars or a four-inch-wide beam.

A good example of a floor programme is to be found in the British Amateur Gymnastics Association's National Development Scheme for Women and Girls. Entering the eighth grade at nine years or over (you work from the eighth to the first grades in the scheme), the compulsory floor exercise requires you to do a tucked backward roll, a cartwheel, splits, a handstand to forward roll, plus a series of steps, hops, jumps, springs, leaps, body waves and various other small connecting movements. The important thing is that you must always be doing something during the minute to a minute and a half you are working on the floor.

Because you are free in floorwork to roam around in a wide open space does not mean you can relax or make it up as you go along. Far from it. You must work as hard on the floor as on the other fixtures of apparatus and you must discipline yourself just the same against certain temptations of seemingly easy ways of trying for marks.

The major temptation is to be too theatrical or, as they say on the stage, 'to play to the gods'. This simply means that you are deliberately appealing for applause by sudden poses and halts in your routine.

The floor exercise, in fact, contains many elements of basic dancing. The progression is from primary foot positions and movements to acrobatics which to the gymnast are back flips, round-offs, somersaults, walkovers, and splits. By contrast, in the theatre and the circus the progression from basic acrobatics (which you will eventually learn) is to contortionism, and the dictionary will tell you plainly what that means: 'to twist with violence, to wrench, to distort'. Your floor exercises must never be the art of twisting your body into weird shapes. If you want to do that you should become a tumbler or trapeze artist in the big top.

Contortionism is most certainly *not* gymnastics because it means extending your body joints beyond their limits. Your floor exercise is to show the judges that you have mobility without irrational posing and that your movements can flow without deliberate pauses. You will get more rewarding applause if your work is artistic rather than showy and it will benefit your marks too. Your judges are sitting on chairs, not heaps of sawdust, so you must not try to impress them with overacting or circus tricks.

To help you on the floor you have the added dimension of music. Unfortunately your accompaniment cannot be a full orchestra and you must be satisfied with music played by one instrument. This is a great pity from your point of view as well as for the spectator of your work because swelling music from a large orchestra can be such an inspiration for co-ordinated movement. However, make the most of the musical assistance because you have to work 'cold' (even after a warm-up) on the other three pieces of apparatus.

The vital thing is that you must feel the music in all your movements, and your personality must be expressed in it. This is your greatest opportunity for self-expression.

Your choice of music is a thing you must discuss at great length with your coach because he or she knows that to be successful on the floor, you must like the melody. It is for you to choose, or at least for you to accept, a piece of music, because if you hate your music you will never work on the floor happily. If you have a feeling for a certain piece of music, or one day you hear a piece for the first time that stirs you inside, then tell your coach immediately.

There is no restriction to your choice, but don't forget your whole floor exercise must not exceed one minute thirty seconds. Don't let that affect your preference because if you are mad about a piece of music which is too long, it can be adapted by taking out phrases and key signatures can be changed if necessary.

The chance of a pianist accompanying your floor exercise in this country is just about nil. It will probably be a tape recording and your coach will sort out the technicalities with you. As only one instrument can be used, it will almost certainly be a piano recording. Make sure that a few notes of music can act as an intro to your piece or, failing that, some sound can be taped to indicate the start of your exercise. It can be very unnerving not knowing exactly when to start the first move.

Tape recorders sometimes go wrong, or it is found at the last moment that the cassette will not fit the equipment. Give a lot of thought beforehand to this because you don't want your work spoiled by mechanical trouble.

Music-wise, you can choose from pop to classical, from baroque to musical comedy and jazz. Nadia Comaneci (Rumania) has performed her floor exercises to pop music but the elegant Elvira Saadi (USSR) works, as you might expect, to something a little more classical—the Habanera from Bizet's *Carmen*. In our opinion, one of the most moving floor exercises ever seen was by the world champion Ludmila Tourischeva (USSR) in the World Cup at Wembley in 1975 when she ended lifeless like the dying puppet in Stravinsky's ballet *Petrouchka*. Her

3 During her sparkling career, Ludmila Tourischeva (USSR) won Olympic, World and European titles, and epitomized the blend of art, theatre and superb gymnastic ability on the floor exercise which took her to the top.

whole routine worked up to this great finale and it was, we thought, good theatre and good gymnastics. The two can go together but such an exercise must be handled with exquisite artistry.

The music that fires you to expression and movement will be of no use to you whatsoever, though, if you fail to appreciate that all artists have to be developed from the raw material of their natural talents. Only by hard work will you ever achieve what you want to do.

Today you see your international heroes and heroines on television doing series of back flips and somersaults, aerial cartwheels and walkovers. It all looks so simple that you feel sure you can do them straightaway simply from the inspiration of watching the greats. But it is not possible, tempting though it may be to try. Those great gymnasts started the same way as you have to, and they worked on the basic moves for a long time before they were ever allowed to do a back flip. Even now they are still liable to make mistakes, and under the pressure of competition before thousands of people, they often do.

At first the purpose of your daily exercises will be to create tension in your body muscles with particular attention to those which are slack in everyday life. There must be tension in your back, stomach, seat and thighs for all the movements you will do on the floor and on the other apparatus.

Suppleness is vital too, and your coach will tell you what daily exercises must be done to achieve this. Never be afraid to ask what every exercise is for. Find out which muscles are being worked upon because it is vital that you should know a lot about the functioning of your body.

Later, when you get on to the more difficult things you will need to know 'where you are'. That is to say, what position your body is in during flight, swings and jumps. You will not, of course, *see* the positions of your body as you move around with rapidity, yet you will have to correct approaching faults by applying pressure to your muscles.

For you to be among the high marks your mind must be the master of your body and, when you get to that advanced stage in your development, you will feel the satisfaction of achievement and the elation of knowing exactly 'where you are going'.

And so, after a period of apprentice training, you will start on your first agility—the Handstand.

Handstand

The first lesson on the handstand is to make sure you have the correct stance because you cannot stand on your hands properly until you know how to stand on your feet. It sounds so easy, but just look around you in everyday life and observe the different ways people stand! The gymnast must stand erect without the stomach or bottom sticking out; the head must be up, arms straight down by the sides, no pike (that is, no forward bend of the trunk) and no hollow (backward inclination of the body). The front of the body from nose to toe will be a straight line and the back likewise, apart from the natural fold between the shoulder and bottom. Now you are ready to start the handstand.

A firm balance on your flat feet is achieved by the body weight (not your actual body) moving slightly forward to your toes, which will act as stabilizers. If you lean back on your heels you will be off balance and will need a backward step to correct the fault.

Now move the arms absolutely straight above your head and near to the ears so that there is a straight line through your arms and right through your back to the floor. Take a step forward and bend your thrusting leg (the one you lifted) so that it takes the weight of your body. The important thing is the length of the step and not its height. The foot reaches out in a forward direction, as in Fig. 4.

Your position now is that you are still on your feet with a straight line through the back leg and body, your arms still straight above your head and the forward leg bent rather like a fencer's lunge. The actual body position is now about half-way between the vertical (standing) and flat on your front on the floor. Your next move will take you to the vertical again, when you will be upside down.

Push hard on the thrusting leg (front

foot) and swing the other leg upwards. Your fingers reach the ground first and should be slightly apart to give a web-like base (Fig. 5). The back leg goes up to the vertical first with a strong action and when your hands have reached the floor, the thrusting leg will have straightened and left the floor to join the back leg for the handstand position (Fig. 6). Your eyes will be looking at your fingertips and your hands must be shoulder-width apart.

Forward walkover

The forward walkover needs strength in the back and stomach muscles and the legs, with suppleness in the hip joints and the spine.

You start off standing upright as for the kick to handstand but thereafter the main difference is that your legs go through the splits position and are never together during the move.

First, lunge forward with the right leg

4 (Far left) *Moving towards the handstand, the straight line through the arm, head, body and back leg can be clearly seen. The thrusting left leg has gone firmly forward with a long step to give power for the next movement.*

5 (Centre) *The hands are now on the floor, with the fingers slightly apart to give a base for the handstand. The right leg swings upwards, keeping the straight line through the body, and the left leg is beginning to straighten, ready to join the right leg in a vertical position.*

6 (Left) *The handstand position, with legs together, hands shoulder-width apart, and eyes looking at the fingertips.*

7 (Left) *National champion Avril Lennox demonstrates the forward walkover. At this initial stage the arms, body and left leg are in a straight line, with the right leg stepping forward.*

8 *The hands are now on the ground, with the swinging left leg having come up, and the legs in the splits position.*

10851151

9 (Right) *The shoulders are pressed well back and kept above the hands as the swinging left leg comes down to the ground, and the thrusting right leg remains high.*

An Leabharlann
A
796.41
Ceard Choláiste Réigiún
Leitir Ceanainn

10 *The swinging left leg is now on the ground, with the thrusting right leg now being lowered to join it. Note that it is kept absolutely straight in its descent.*

(Fig. 7) and put your hands straight above your head, covering the ears. At that position the left (swinging) leg will be at the same angle as the body with the floor so that your arms, body and left leg will be in a straight line. Bend forward from the hips to place your hands on the floor as in the handstand.

Your swinging leg now swings upwards and over and when your thrusting leg leaves the ground, your legs should be in the splits position (Fig. 8).

As you go through the splits handstand you must press your shoulders well back and be sure to keep them over your hands and, as the left leg comes down to the ground (Fig. 9) to land, keep the right leg high.

You then return to the standing position with your right leg still as high as possible (Fig. 10).

This move has been traced through starting with the right leg as the thruster and the left as the swinger. It can, of course, be done the other way, starting off with the left leg.

Back flip

Once you have reached proficiency with the handstand and you can comfortably do walkovers and backbends, your coach may start you on a most exciting movement into flight—the back flip.

It is a backward dive from your feet to your hands, and then back to your feet, in which you must sense where you are going because you will not see your path in the primary stage.

But there is no need to fear the agility because you will have mats and you will be supported by your coach.

Furthermore, before you attempt the flic-flac (another name for the back flip) you will have worked on the various parts of the move before putting them together as a complete movement. Courage is needed for this element, and the preparation is all important, but before you actually do a back flip, you must work conscientiously through the various stages. Let us examine these.

First, you must learn a donkey kick. You swing to handstand and then relax the back and legs so that you can snap the legs down to the ground. As you do so, you must push off the hands, keeping the arms by the ears. There will be a moment when the hands and feet are off the floor at the same time before coming to the upright standing position. If this is not achieved, you should not progress any further.

Now for stage two. Stand up straight with your arms by your ears. Fold at the hips and bend the legs so that the body is off balance; swing the arms down. Your coach will be supporting you here, of course, otherwise you would simply sit down. Then from the folded position you open the body so that you are leaning back in a straight line. You must repeat this many times, keeping body tension, and once this little move is perfected you can go on to the next stage.

For stage three, the coach will need to support you with one hand on your neck and the other holding the back of your waist. It will help a great deal if you are wearing tights or trousers so that your coach has something to grip.

Folding the hips again from a standing position and, swinging your arms upwards, you should open the body into a straight line as before but this time jump as you go backwards. Don't try jumping without bending your legs but, at the same time, keep the bend to a minimum. You must keep control of your body in the jump and land back exactly where you started.

Just before you are ready for the back flip proper you may do a move which is not an actual progression to the agility, but which is simply a reminder that you are going backwards on to your hands and then on to your feet. With help from your coach you will bend back to the bridge position and then lift the legs over and to the floor keeping them together.

And so to the actual back flip (Figs. 11–15) when the coach will support you, with a slightly different technique. You will go through the hip folding, then the body straightening as you thrust upwards and backwards from your feet, the bridge position in aerial form as you go over, the donkey kick to snap your feet down from the handstand and, finally, you are back to the upright ready, perhaps, for another back flip. But before performing consecutive back flips, you will need much practice.

11–15 The back flip. From the standing position, the knees bend as if the gymnast is about to sit on a stool, while actually preparing for the spring backwards. The arms are ready to swing forwards and upwards to help the thrust.

12 The dive backwards, which has to be perfected with a coach before you try it on your own. The gymnast goes through the 'bridge' position in aerial form.

13 The hands touch down on the mat with the fingers pointing to the direction from which you have come. The 'bridge' leads into the 'donkey kick', as the legs swing together over the head, and the gymnast pushes down hard on the floor.

14 The 'donkey kick' position brings the legs back towards the upright position, and the hands are leaving the floor.

15 Back to the upright position for the completion of the back flip.

CHAPTER TWO

Vaulting

A vault over the broad horse will take you only about five seconds from the moment you start your run-up to the apparatus to the time you make your final landing on the other side. Put like that it sounds so simple and trivial that you may well think—'I can't make many mistakes in five seconds so I am going to put all my efforts into the asymmetric bars, the ninety-five seconds on the balance beam and the one and a half minutes on my floor exercise'.

A few years ago, twenty maybe, going over the broad horse was more or less a hop, skip and a jump with a sheer drop on the other side. But today you need the combined skills of an athlete and a gymnast before you will become a good vaulter.

Obviously there is less to learn for a mere two or three seconds' journey through the air than there is for routines on the other three disciplines. But never forget that your more advanced vaults will be priced at 10 marks and could give you a 'flying' start, if you will excuse the pun, because in a championship match the horse is likely to be your first piece of apparatus.

So don't make the big mistake early in your gymnastics career of under-rating the vault, or any other piece of apparatus for that matter. They are all of equal importance. Just imagine how you will feel with even, say, 9.25 marks after your first effort in an important championship. It could set you up for a gold medal and a title.

You have one great advantage on the vault which you will not get on the others. You have two attempts and the vault that gets the higher mark counts as your score. This opens up several options – you may go for the difficult one first and, if that fails, you can play safe with an easier second vault. Or if you feel you scored well on a simple first, you may decide for your second attempt to try a difficult one for a higher tariff.

You will hear a lot about 'first' and 'second' flight. Get it firmly into your mind exactly what this is – flight is the 'free' ('free' in gymnastics is when you are not touching anything with any part of your body) moment when you are actually in the air. So first flight is from the time your feet leave the board until your fingers touch the horse and second flight is from the time your fingers leave the horse for the second journey through space *en route* for feet down on the floor to complete the vault.

What is the vital thing in vaulting? Meg Warren, the women's national senior squad coach, answers thus:

'The most important aspect of any vault is the run. If the gymnast cannot run fast she will never be a good vaulter. The young gymnast must pay attention to her running style and speed before she actually starts vaulting practice. The length of the vault run-up must be consistent; there must be no break or change in step. It is good if from the beginning the gymnast uses a tape measure to check on her distance.'

The winners of medals for vaulting in international events and lesser competitions are nearly always those gymnasts who have the fastest run-up.

Mrs Warren continues:

'The gymnast should never attempt a vault that is too difficult for her. It is best for a beginner to work hard at squat vaults. Only when they are perfect should the gymnast go on to a long arm.

'When learning a new vault it must be broken down so that when the final skill is to be tackled very little assistance is required from the coach. If the build-up is slow, so that the gymnast understands every stage, then she will feel confident and able to work with greater knowledge of her movements, even though she is travelling fast.'

So, after the squat vaults your objective will be the long-arm overthrow, the first of the basic inverted (upside-down) vaults. In the long arm you are required to jump from the Reuther springboard to a handstand on the horse and then to lift off with straight arms to land on the other side with your back to the horse.

But before you ever attempt the long arm you will be working on basics for perhaps a year – maybe even longer. When a singer starts training she does not immediately sing 'One Fine Day' from *Madam Butterfly*, nor does a ballet dancer perform 'The Dying Swan' until after many years of basic training. Many young people try to jump the gun but they will never succeed without a sound background of groundwork. The singer may do nothing but scales for years, and the dancer practises her foot positions, sautés and relevés, day in and day out. The same thing goes for the gymnast, and on the horse the progression is to perfect your run and then your squat and straddle vaults. You can then go on to the handstand vaults which are the threshold of new and exciting experiences. In gymnastics there are always new experiences ahead, but you must never fail to consolidate at every stage before going on to the next.

Long-arm overthrow

At the start of training for the long-arm overthrow (Figs. 16–19) you will be back to the Reuther board practice for the first flight, which is forwards and upwards with much more thrust and power than you have been accustomed to on the horizontal vaults. Your coach will be close to you as always in the early stages of all new moves and, in this one, she will support you at all the critical phases of the vault. She will also decide the distance of the Reuther board from the horse and the length of your run-up. (In your gym you will have either the Reuther board, which has a padded top, or the bare springboard of slatted wood.)

You start running and must get to top speed as soon as possible. The last step that takes you to the board will be higher and longer than the rest and you must aim to land on the board just below where it flattens out at the top. Look closely at the board and you will see that it slopes upwards and away from you as you run up and, near the top, it flattens out. You must make for the top of the slope.

Taking off from one foot you land on the Reuther board with both feet firmly together but those same two feet of yours must be slightly in front of your body, which means your body will be tilted slightly backwards. The tilt will disappear automatically in the split second that you are on the board.

At this point don't bend your legs more than necessary. Your toes touch down first (a basic principle of all vaulting), followed by your heels, and you take off immediately with your heels, leaving your toes as the final aid to thrust into the first flight of your journey into space. Both your arms must swing together from behind your body, forward and upward as forcefully as you can make them to increase the power of your lift-off.

Until you have practised the long-arm-overthrow vault you can't be too precise about the angle of contact with the horse. But you should touch down just before the vertical – if you land at a higher angle or beyond the vertical you will almost certainly fall forward without much hope for the second flight.

The horse is a departure platform where you will simply thrust upwards and outwards with a completely straight body so that your arms, head, body and legs in the extended position will pass through the horizontal with the ceiling and floor.

In this layout position (your body must be absolutely straight) you will be like a magician's stooge, floating on air without any visible means of support. But you won't be on a magic carpet, because your stay there won't exceed a thousandth part of a second.

If you have done everything correctly you will now be homing towards the mat beyond the broad horse to make your landing from outer space with your body as straight as a space rocket (arms above head, body and legs in an absolutely straight line) at an angle of about 60 degrees backwards from the vertical.

The angle will be less on landing and you will bend the knees a little to reduce the impact (Fig. 19) and your arms stay above your head as the body moves up to the vertical.

You might end the exercise with a slight flourish but don't overdo it. If you have done the vault well the audience will applaud you for execution rather than for an excess of 'show-off' at the end of it.

16–19 The long-arm overthrow, demonstrated by Avril Lennox. Here Avril has sprung from the Reuther board, and with a straight body and a low trajectory, resulting from a fast heel lift on the board, is about to touch down on the horse.

17 Now the horse becomes a departure platform, as Avril hollows her back in the handstand position ready for the powerful thrust-off for the second flight of the vault.

18 The thrust from the horse has given the straight, stretched position to the body.

19 The straight body position must be maintained until the knees bend on landing to cushion the impact. The body is finally straightened again to complete the exercise.

Yamashita

In gymnastics, moves are frequently named after the gymnast who first performed them, and your next goal on the broad horse will probably be one of them – the Yamashita (Figs. 20–24). This was first seen at the Olympics in Tokyo in 1964 when Haruhiro Yamashita of Japan surprised everyone with a long arm in the first flight, followed by a deep pike in the second.

In a few words, the Yamashita is a handspring off the horse to an immediate pike, followed by full extension of the body before landing. There are at the most three twisting refinements of the move but they will come later. The advance of gymnastics can be measured by the fact that whereas the straight Yamashita was worth 10 marks in 1964, it is now worth only 9.40 marks for women. A Yamashita with half a turn during the second flight off the horse now has a full tariff of 10 marks, but from January, 1978, it is worth 9.60 marks.

So you can see, there is a lot of consolidating work to be done on the horse before you will qualify for top marks. In fact, the long arm we discussed at length is marked at 9.20 and there is no way of getting more for that vault, because the tariff laid down in the

Federation Internationale de Gymnastique (FIG) Code of Points is the absolute maximum.

Your run-up for the Yamashita is as in the long-arm overthrow, and you take off with legs closed and straight. From the Reuther board you must go through a front layout (horizontal position in the air) and, just before your fingers touch the horse, you must be half-way between the horizontal and the vertical.

In the first phase of the long-arm overthrow you go to the inverted vertical (upside down on your hands), but in the Yamashita you will not reach the actual straight handstand.

Soon after your hands touch the horse from the first flight, your hips start moving and, with the thrust off, your chest begins moving towards your feet for the deep pike which is characteristic of this vault in its second flight. In fact, the sooner you commence body flexion towards the pike the sooner will you start the body extension of the second flight. A late pike will lead to a late extension,

20–24 Avril Lennox demonstrates the Yamashita vault. Note the hollow back position as she approaches the horse, which has resulted from a fast heel kick at take-off. The legs are closed and straight, and she is rising to a position half-way between the horizontal and the vertical.

21 (Above) *When you are near a vertical position with your hands on the horse, the hips begin to move ready for the pike and, with the thrust-off, the chest starts moving towards the feet for the deep pike position.*

22 (Above, right) *An excellent example of a good pike. Anything deeper would make it difficult to reach the full extension shown in Fig. 23.*

23 (Opposite, above) *The legs, still together, thrust sharply away from the pike into the stretch position, with the arms behind the gymnast and maximum body extension.*

24 (Opposite, below) *To conclude the vault, the knees bend to cushion the impact on landing. The finishing stance shows the body erect, the back hollowed, and the arms straight above the head, covering the ears.*

followed by over-rotation and a poor landing.

The exact degree of pike is not laid down, but the minimum must be 90 degrees (that is the letter L, legs to body) while the maximum is near to the legs touching the chest.

Your thrust must be very powerful because the body and arms are lifting upwards towards your feet as you go into the second flight and the pike must be accomplished at the highest point of the second flight.

From the deep pike you must thrust your legs forward sharply through the L position towards a full extension of the body with your arms behind you. Continue towards the floor in this extended position and when you actually land you will be possibly 10 to 15 degrees backwards from the vertical. On the point of impact with the floor your knees will bend so as to cushion the landing, and you finish standing erect with your arms above your head and by the ears.

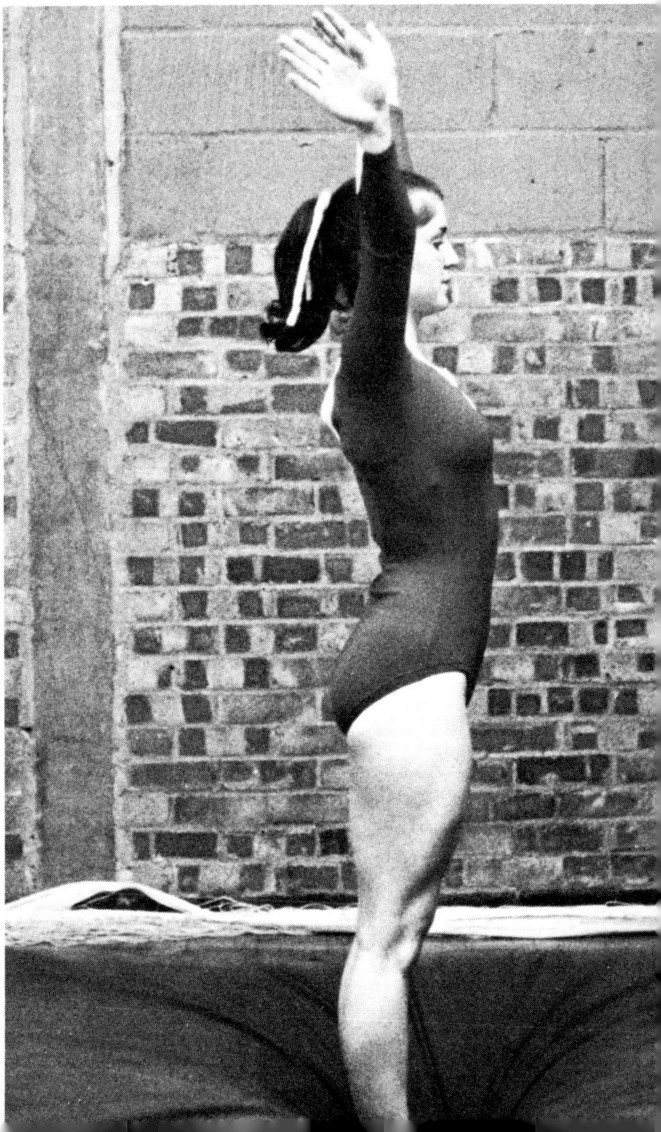

Tsukahara

Now for a quick look at a more advanced vault, the Tsukahara (Figs. 25–29), which is also named after the Japanese gymnast who first performed it.

When Haruhiro Yamashita first did his piked spring into second flight at Tokyo in 1964, it was hailed as a new move of great difficulty. Now it has become so commonplace that one wonders if the same thing will happen to the Tsukahara. Will the very young gymnast starting on her basic training reach the Tsukahara sooner than today's top gymnasts? Will it become just another low-tariff vault?

When you look back on the progress of all sports over the last ten years, the mind boggles at what may happen in the next decade. We think that even more difficult moves and records are impossible, but we are invariably proved wrong. We can suppose, just as in show jumping, that apparatus might be placed higher, or women gymnasts might work the long horse instead of the broad.

However, let us stick to the present day, when only about six British women are doing the Tsukahara – the vault that demands a quarter or half turn on to the horse, followed by a one-and-a-half somersault in the second flight.

25–29 The Tsukahara vault, demonstrated by Olympic representative Susan Cheesebrough, calls for an over-rotated cartwheel on to the horse (a quarter turn plus) and the rest, to complete a half turn of the body, is done on the horse. Here Susan has over-rotated the cartwheel well going on, thus reducing the amount of turn needed before the somersault.

26 The half turn has now been completed, and she thrusts into the back somersault by drawing up the knees. Once committed at this point you cannot change course.

Physically it is not much more difficult than some of the other vaults, but it calls for far greater courage. Once you are committed to the back somersault, you cannot adjust your course.

One thing is certain; you will not be called for a Tsukahara until you have perfected the others, so don't be afraid that your coach will suddenly ask you to take risks.

27 With national coach Bill McLoughlin watching for any dangerous mistakes, the back somersault continues . . .

28 . . . until Susan turns right over in the tucked position . . .

29 . . . to eventually land feet first, facing the horse.

CHAPTER THREE

Beam

Now we come to the tight-rope of gymnastics – the balance beam. It calls for courage, an ice-cold nerve, good poise and posture, and complete control of balance to keep yourself steady on a padded plank of wood four inches wide and six inches deep, four feet up from the ground and sixteen feet long.

In one sense this piece of apparatus is an extension of the floor because all the basics you are learning there will also be worked on the beam. But you must master the floor agilities before you try them on the beam.

The Federation Internationale de Gymnastique (the world governing body for gymnastics) Code of Points states very clearly what is expected of you. It is an exercise of balance with acrobatics and gymnastics movements in which you are required to make many journeys up and down the entire length of the beam during the course of a routine. You will learn pivots, leaps, jumps, hops, steps and running combinations and you will be required to work in a crouched or squat position as well as standing upright.

The duration of your exercise in a competition will be between one minute fifteen seconds and one minute thirty-five seconds. Timekeeping starts from the second your feet leave the floor or springboard, and the watch stops when your feet touch the ground again on the completion of your exercise.

There will be a warning whistle or bell at one minute thirty seconds and again at one minute thirty-five seconds. If you leave it until the last second to dismount, it will be all right provided you spring from the beam on the stroke of the final warning.

Nothing you do after one minute thirty-five seconds will count towards your marks. In fact, just the reverse; you will lose 0.30 of a mark for exceeding the time limit. You will also lose 0.05 for every second short of the minimum one minute fifteen seconds. So you will realize that later on you have to consider the content of your routine not only in terms of elements of difficulty but also in relation to a fairly strict timetable.

If you fall from the beam you lose 0.50 of a mark and you must re-mount within ten seconds. If you leave it longer, then your exercise is considered finished.

Timekeeping does not stop whilst you are off the beam, so it is to your advantage to get back as soon as possible.

You may remember a warning on the floor exercise about 'playing to the gods' for applause. Well, here again you must not be too theatrical – no stopping for effect or to steady your balance after acrobatic elements. However, apart from a fleeting pause for an arabesque or a balance, three brief stops are allowed, but they must not disturb the rhythm of your exercise nor should they precede, follow or be included in a move of medium or superior difficulty.

Your coach will first tell you to walk up and down the full length of the beam until you find yourself doing it as naturally as walking on the ground. Then you will go on to pirouettes, half turns on one foot to put you in a reverse direction, and then the full turn of 360 degrees.

This preparatory work is absolutely vital because so often even the most experienced gymnast can suddenly fall from the beam and you can tell by the expression on her face that it was a complete surprise. For the experienced gymnast it is usually before, during or after a particularly difficult superior move but it will happen to you in simple elements if you fail to do enough walking and running and turning and jumping.

How much practice is enough? Well, the simple answer is you cannot have enough practice. The world's top gymnasts do the basics daily, just as you should.

The beam has a parallel in cricket where a batsman on a good pitch looks as safe as houses. But he knows only too well at the back of his mind that just one slip of concentration or a simple mistake can send him back to the dressing room. For that innings he is finished. At least you can mount the beam again, but it will have cost you 0.50 marks and that is probably more than enough to put you out of contention in any championship.

So it is concentration that makes a good beam routine, given that everything else is equal. If you watch the experienced gymnast you will notice she is thinking very hard as she walks gracefully along the beam.

The beam has a particular problem of its own – you have got to get on to it. On the floor you walk on, strike a pose and wait for the music. On the broad horse, entry and exit are all part of a single exercise that is over in a flash. But on bars and beam you have to mount, and the beam mount means you have to lift yourself up from the ground to your four-inch-wide working area, four feet up.

Your broad-horse training for vaults is going to be useful now because nearly all mounts require a vault – that is to say, you will run and then spring from your feet. Once on the way, your hands will contact the beam to give you balance.

Forward roll mount

The forward roll on to the end of the beam is an exciting mount and it is also quite spectacular from the audience's point of view. It is a very fast move and the speed of the roll helps you along to a standing position on the beam. But whatever you do, avoid making the 'roll' and 'stand up' into two distinct elements. It is all one movement.

Stand facing either end of the beam

30 Beginning the forward roll on to the beam. The hands and arms are parallel to allow the thumbs to come together on the top of the four-inch-wide beam.

31 The arms straighten, the hands push hard on the beam, and the body is lifted so that the seat is high. The body is now in a deep pike position, with arms bent, and the head is tucked under ready for the roll.

and spring from a Reuther board (or without one) from both feet. Place your hands so that the thumbs of both hands are together (Fig. 30). With your arms straight and pushing hard on the beam, you lift your body so that the seat is high and the legs are at about 30 degrees from the horizontal. The legs will lift higher as the roll continues (Fig. 31).

You must now tuck your head under

32 The roll goes through the shoulders and spine, to the seat. The spine is curved throughout, and you are never lying flat on your back on the beam.

33 The momentum of the roll has taken the gymnast into a sitting position. The right leg is bent with the heel close to the seat. The shoulders should come forward to assist the move from sitting to standing position with the weight on the right leg. The whole sequence from Figs. 30–33 and to standing upright should be one consecutive movement.

as your arms bend and the roll must go from the shoulders right through the spine to your seat (Fig. 32). Your shoulders come forward as you move from the sitting to the standing position (Fig. 33).

It is best to stand up by bending one leg, bringing the heel close in to the seat and stretching the other leg forwards to finally stand with the weight on it.

Cartwheel

A cartwheel on the beam (Figs. 34–37) sounds somewhat fearsome but if you have learned the move in a perfectly straight line on the floor, then the beam wheel should not cause you too much concern. In any case, you will first be taught the movement on the low beam, so don't have any sleepless nights anticipating problems.

Just as on the floor-exercise cartwheel, you can go on to either hand but don't forget that eventually you will want the choice of right or left. Your arms and legs must be straight throughout the movement and if you can visualize a large wooden wheel of a cart (from which the movement takes its name) with four spokes, then you will see clearly in your mind's eye what you are attempting.

Practise the cartwheel on a line on the floor and practise it many times until you find yourself travelling all the way along the straight line. Remember that it is easier to start the cartwheel on the beam facing front (that is to say, looking straight down the beam) so in your floor practices start it that way.

Next go on to a bench about ten inches wide such as you will find at school. Continue to maintain good extension and body tension.

34–37 The cartwheel on beam. The gymnast is facing down the length of the beam as the lungeing left leg goes forward, and the left arm moves down because the left hand will be first to touch the beam.

5 (Above) *The left hand has touched down a few* *oments before the right hand, with the fingers pointing* *owards the wall (i.e. behind the cartwheel), and the right* *g lifting towards the splits position.*

6 (Below) *Supported by both hands, the gymnast goes* *rough the splits position with the right leg swinging* *ver to begin the return to upright.*

37 Returning to the upright position, with the gymnast facing the way she came.

If you have worked through these stages conscientiously you are now ready for the floor (low) beam. It is an apparatus lifted a few inches from the ground and need not necessarily be sixteen feet long. When regular success is achieved with good style and control, then you are ready to try the skill on the high beam and, if you have progressed properly, the exercise should be perfectly easy and safe.

If, however, you have been cutting corners and if you have not concentrated on extension, style and control, then you are likely to make mistakes and hurt yourself. Gymnastics is very safe if performed correctly.

Free cartwheel

For the free cartwheel on the beam (Figs. 38–42), your direction must again be in an absolutely straight line because your landing strip is only four inches wide and the slightest deviation means you will almost certainly fall off. You will not be asked to try the exercise until you can do the ordinary cartwheel on the beam, by which time the element of fear will be greatly reduced.

When you go through the lunge position you must have lots of spring from the thrusting leg because height is of the utmost importance. A powerful thrust is essential (Figs. 38–39), then the secret of the move lies in co-ordination between the swinging leg and the thrusting leg.

Unlike the straight legs of the handstand/handspring move, you go through the splits position in the free cartwheel (Fig. 40). To assist the movement your arms can swing backwards and you should watch the beam as you turn over.

The commonest fault is a lack of leg thrust and too little swing from the other leg.

38–42 The free cartwheel on the beam. This is more difficult than the ordinary cartwheel, because there is no hand support. The gymnast starts in the same way, facing down the length of the beam with one foot forward. But the arms are outstretched in preparation for the swing.

39 The left (thrusting) leg is anchored to the beam for a powerful thrust as the right (swinging) leg comes up.

40 The right leg swings over so that the body passes in a sideways move through the air, and showing the splits position.

41 The swinging right leg has landed first, and the gymnast balances with the arms as the left leg comes through. Note that in all the pictures the gymnast is watching the beam.

42 The completion of the free cartwheel on the beam.

43 The beam exercise must include elements of balance, and here Avril Lennox demonstrates the 'stag balance', which is one possibility for a beam routine. The hands are either side of the beam, with the thumbs pressing on it from the top, as in the forward roll mount. Note the straight line from the hands to the hips, as one leg is kept straight and the other bent inwards for the 'stag'.

CHAPTER FOUR

Asymmetric Bars

The fourth piece of apparatus is the asymmetric bars, also known as the high and low bars, or the uneven parallel bars. The latter name is probably the most descriptive because although the two bars are parallel, they are not the same height. The high one is 230 cm (7 feet 6 inches) from the ground and the low bar is 150 cm (4 feet 7 inches).

You will not see a great deal of the bars in your first days in the gymnasium. Body preparation will be the first priority and these physical exercises will apply to the future work on all four pieces of apparatus. It will only be as you develop your strength and suppleness, that you will be introduced to the more complicated bar work.

The need for body-strength training is vital. Strength is your dynamo and you really want more than you will normally use to act as a reserve power when you have to correct errors in your routine. You require strength in all parts of your body and particularly in the back, legs, stomach and shoulders. But don't aim to become Miss Atlas!

Bill McLoughlin, senior coach to the British Amateur Gymnastics Association, says:

'Exercises on the asymmetric bars involve mainly swing, although body tension and strength are very important, especially for the skills which involve flight between the bars and going to the handstand.

'It is the hardest piece of apparatus for girls to master, and most of the basic training concentrates on learning to swing correctly and on short circle work, like the mill circle. Most of this can, of course, be learnt on a single bar such as a low horizontal.

'This is a great advantage to the very young and small gymnast who, purely because of size, will find great difficulty in wrapping round the low bar from the high bar.'

Always remember there is no time for fooling about when you are under instruction, although that does not mean training is a grim and boring business. Laughter will mingle with tears and frustration with success, but there will only be frustration if you do not observe strict discipline at all times in the gymnasium.

Right from the start you will become aware of discipline through your coach. It is the very essence of gymnastics – not purely for safety reasons, but as the only way of learning skills and progressing in the sport. You will fail utterly without it.

One rigid discipline on the bars which you will learn immediately concerns the protection of your hands. There are hand straps specially made for gymnasts and you must learn to wear these right from the beginning. Your coach will be most particular about this and will instruct you on the correct way of putting them on and will make regular inspections of your hands to ensure all is well.

There will be chalk in the gym – actually it is magnesium carbonate and *not* French chalk, as is sometimes believed. French chalk is mentioned here as a warning because *on no account should it be used*; it is too slippery.

Before going to the bars chalk the palms of your hands, but don't dip them into the soft white substance in the way you would with water in a wash basin. You will find it is messy enough just applying it to your palms. 'Chalk' is mainly to absorb hand perspiration, but it also helps to counteract friction.

If you start developing callouses then you must grease your hands using Vaseline and hand creams, but be careful which ones you use. Your coach will advise you on this but don't forget he may be a very busy person who is training hundreds of other gymnasts, so you must report any hand complaints without waiting to be asked.

Watch the experienced gymnast going to the bars. First she examines the distance between the high and low bar and makes any adjustments needed. There are two handles for this and they will move both bars forward or backward to suit your 'bar width' (the distance between the bars that suits you best). She then looks carefully at the position of the mats and, finally, before getting into position to await the green flag (or light or hand signal) from the chief judge, she goes to the powder bowl to chalk her palms. The straps she is wearing make her hands slightly cupped.

Once again, watching the experienced gymnast (and this is a thing you must do as often as possible), you will observe the speed with which she flies between the bars. She flies and catches with the rapidity of a monkey at the zoo which, because it has little weight, can fly around almost like a bird.

The weight of your body will be balanced by your strength so that you too can fly rapidly between the bars in the same way as the ape goes from branch to branch. You must imitate the ape too in minimum use of stops and pauses. Rarely will you see such an animal stop before a difficult jump. There may be only the tiniest of pauses as it looks quickly to see where its next move is to be.

The judges will allow a fully fledged gymnast in competition an almost imperceptible pause before an element of difficulty. But that slight break must seem natural and should never advertise the fact that you are about to try something difficult.

The penalty for a definite stop is 0.20 of a mark. You will lose half a mark for falling off the bars and the same penalty for an extra swing of the legs. So you must move from one skill to the next without any of the pauses or poses you are allowed on the floor and beam.

Mill circle

And now to a move you will learn early in your bars training – the mill circle. This skill should only be attempted at the direction of your coach who will help you in all your first attempts.

The forward circle starts with your legs at about seventeen to eighteen minutes past eight o'clock (straddle support, Fig. 44) or as near to the splits as possible. Your hands will be in reverse grip – that is, with the fingers pointing backwards (hands and legs are on the same bar).

44 The straddle support position, prior to the mill circle. With hands in the reverse grip (fingers pointing backwards) and legs in the splits position, the body is lifted off the bar and the weight transferred to the hands and straight arms.

45 The leading leg reaches forward to make the circle as long as possible, with hips well forward and head high. The legs must be wide in circling the bar.

The actual forward mill circle begins when you lift the body off the bar and thus transfer the weight on to your hands with absolutely straight arms. The leading leg (it can be left or right according to how your legs were at straddle support) should be stretched forward into the void ahead of you (Fig. 45) with the hips well forward and the head high. Your legs must be wide as you go round the bar.

Your head must be held up throughout the move and your body extended as you start to rise from your journey down below. Stretch the thrusting leg (forward one) over the bar (Fig. 46) as you come back to where you started at straddle support.

Upstart between the bars

Among the many problems on the bars is getting your body from a position under

46 The forward leg is now coming up behind the bar and is stretched, still straight, over it to complete the full mill circle.

a bar to above it. The name of the move that accomplishes this is the upstart – a fairly self-explanatory term – and the action of the move calls for body strength combined with split-second timing of your arm movements.

You start absolutely straight with your body at full stretch, hands holding the top bar in ordinary grasp (that is, fingers pointing towards the low bar) and with your seat on the low bar (Fig. 47). For this back-support position, you will have to adjust the bars to your width.

Remember you have no preparatory swing on the upstart between the bars. The first move is simply a swing of the legs downwards whilst extending your shoulders. This places your shoulders far away from the vertical of the top bar.

Now lift your toes rapidly to the top bar thus freeing your seat from the low bar which means you are swinging backwards (Fig. 48). You really have to work fast because you are so restricted in swinging movements in this skill.

The toes continue moving upwards and the bar travels down the front of the thighs (Fig. 49). You are now opening the angle in the hips and closing the one between your arms and chest. The pulling-down action of the arms is very vital and you will need much strength in that region to succeed.

As the bar travels down your thighs so the feet will move downwards until the bar comes to the groin. In order to get the bar to this position the arms must bend according to the difference in length of the gymnast's body and arms.

Once you have got to this position your whole body then goes through the end of a forward circle movement keeping the same pike (that is, fold of the legs and body at the hips). Ensure the arms are flexed and the hips are into the bar.

This position on the bar (Fig. 50) is vital if you are going to make a swing-away movement to take you straight into the next skill.

47–50 Upstart between the bars. The body is straight as a poker, with the seat on the lower bar and the hands gripping the upper bar in ordinary grasp.

48 The toes are lifted rapidly above the top bar and a backwards swing begins.

49 The bar is pressed strongly down the legs, closing the angle between the arms and trunk, and straightening the body angle at the hips.

50 (Opposite) *The straightened body is now swung to the front support position above the top bar.*

Dislocation catch

You start this move in front support on the top bar, facing the low bar. The first movement is to raise your body and hips from the bar (lay off, Fig. 51) into a long swing. During the long swing the body remains straight and as it passes under the high bar the hips begin to lead the swing. When your hips make contact with the low bar the legs continue to swing forward into as deep a pike as possible (Fig. 52). At this point the hands are released from the top bar and swing downwards and forwards. Your legs continue to come round to complete the full circle on the low bar (Fig. 53).

This is the critical moment, for now

51–55 (Left to right) *Susan Cheesebrough demonstrates the dislocation catch. The body and hips are swung from a front support position above the top bar into a 'lay-off', ready for a long swing.*

52 *The long swing goes under the top bar, and the hips contact the lower bar with the legs straight and the body going into a deep pike position. Note that the hands have left the top bar.*

53 *The body wraps around the lower bar until a powerful thrust from the hips (Fig. 54) sends the gymnast backwards and upwards.*

you spring from the thighs upwards and backwards and to accomplish this the body moves rapidly from the pike into an arched (hollow) position. The arms are turned outwards with the hands and fingers pointing backwards (Fig. 54).

At this point you cannot see which way you are going because you are travelling backwards and upwards. But your coach will be watching you very carefully to ensure your safety should you miss the top bar.

From the spring from your thighs, the top of your head should rise to a position above the bar and your reversed hands must also be above so that you can drop downwards on to the bar for the catch (Fig. 55).

54–55 The body begins to move from the previous pike to an arched (hollow) position as the thrust from the thighs pushes the gymnast towards the top bar. The arms turn outwards with the hands and fingers pointing backwards, and the thrust should send the top of the head slightly above the higher bar so that the gymnast is virtually dropping down towards it for the final catch.

CHAPTER FIVE

Other Fields

No book, however thick, can hope to cover the complete range of such a diverse sport as gymnastics. Each of the separate pieces of apparatus deserves a book to itself, and we can do no more than describe some of the basic moves you will need to master in each case. However, perhaps just a brief word about some of the other aspects of the sport would not be amiss.

Modern rhythmic gymnastics

A relatively new but rapidly expanding part of the sport, modern rhythmic gymnastics, has a very marked influence from the world of dancing, especially ballet. It is really an extension of the floor exercise, and shuns any major apparatus like bars or vaulting horses. However, it does introduce small items of hand apparatus, such as a rope, hoop, ball, ribbon or clubs, and these can be an essential part of the exercise, which is performed to music.

The body and apparatus must be co-ordinated practically as one, and the exercise must show a wide variety of dance steps, jumps, leaps, balances, turns and pivots, with a demonstration of flexibility and co-ordination. Good interpretation of the music, both in choreography and pace, is essential.

The modern rhythmic gymnast has three basic sections from which to choose: solo exercise with hand apparatus; solo exercise without hand apparatus; or group exercise.

Using hand apparatus, the solo gymnast can employ elements of medium or superior difficulty, as set out in an International Code of Points, but the essential thing is to keep the apparatus constantly moving, whether it is a ball, rope, ribbon, or whatever. It must never be held still when the body is moving, and it must be manipulated with the left hand as well as the right to achieve balance of composition.

The solo exercise without apparatus is really almost a dance routine, which should exhibit great suppleness, as well as the other components previously

56 (Opposite) *A ball is just one item of hand apparatus that can be used in modern rhythmic gymnastics.*

mentioned, within a time limit of one minute thirty seconds (minimum) to two minutes (maximum).

The group exercise is performed by a team of six gymnasts, using hand apparatus which they must exchange between themselves at least four times during the two and a half to three minute exercise. They also have to form no less than six different formations, but acrobatic elements, as in the solo exercises, are forbidden. The group is marked both on the composition of its programme and the actual performance. Modern rhythmic gymnastics has long been a part of the sport in Europe, and the first world championships, held in 1963, were dominated by the Eastern bloc. In 1975 Great Britain took part in the world championships, held in Madrid, for the first time.These championships are held on alternate years, and there is also the possibility of the sport becoming part of the Olympic programme in the future.

Sports acrobatics

Another branch of gymnastics with a possible Olympic future, and which is quickly gaining popularity in Britain, is sports acrobatics. Here, teamwork between two or more people is the vital ingredient. A sports acrobatics committee of the B.A.G.A. was formed in July 1975, and the following year the inaugural British national championships were staged at Huddersfield with separate categories for men's pairs; women's pairs; mixed pairs; women's threes; and men's fours.

It calls for even less apparatus than modern rhythmic gymnastics, and competitions are staged using just the standard twelve-metre-square floor exercise area, but training can take place virtually anywhere: in a gym, on grass, indoors or outside.

The aim of sports acrobatics is to show relationship in movement, supporting a partner, and executing moves which could not be done on your own. A number of gymnasts who came into the sport rather late for apparatus success are now among those finding an opportunity for expression and fulfilment through sports acrobatics.

Again, the Eastern Europeans already have the sport down to a fine art. The Soviet Display Team at Wembley has several times demonstrated just what can be achieved, particularly through the talents of the world men's pairs champions, Vladimir Alimanov and Vladimir Nazarov – 'The Two Vladimirs'.

Tumbling is a rather more established part of sports acrobatics, and Britain has already obtained a fair degree of success internationally, ever since Morgan Smith of Leeds was a finalist in the first world championships at Moscow in 1974.

57 (Opposite) *The world pairs champions in sports acrobatics, the Soviet Union's 'Two Vladimirs', in an exhibition at Wembley.*

72 71

B.A.G.A. awards scheme

Many youngsters may never actually take part in a gymnastics competition as such, but a most successful awards scheme has been in operation in Britain since 1971, organized by the British Amateur Gymnastics Association and sponsored by *The Sunday Times*. This scheme concentrates on personal improvement rather than setting one gymnast against another competitively.

The scheme is simply based on the ability to perform a number of exercises, beginning with a series of ten comparatively simple ones which should be within the range of most children. By adequately performing a minimum of any six out of the ten (which include such things as a forward roll, and a leapfrog over a partner) the child qualifies for the Grade 4 award, which includes a certificate and a coloured sew-on badge suitable for the tracksuit or leotard.

By achieving six out of the ten exercises laid down for the next award, the child can then progress to Grade 3, and so on, right up to the top award, Grade 1, for which a handspring, splits or rear vault are among the requisite exercises. In each case the test is adjudicated by a club coach or school teacher, who then sends off for the necessary certificate or badge. The six exercises do *not* all have to be performed on the same day.

The success of the scheme was such that within a short time of its launch, thousands of schools had taken it up as part of their PE programme, aided by special wall-charts, group achievement charts, and personal achievement cards, which the coach or teacher fills in. By November 1974 – just over three years after its launch – a total of *one million* badges had been distributed among young gymnasts around Britain, and in March 1977 this total moved beyond two million.

The excellence of this graduated scheme lies in the fact that no child need feel defeated by another. Success depends entirely on his or her own efforts. Full details of the scheme, its awards and its requirements, can be obtained from the British Amateur Gymnastics Association, 23A High Street, Slough, Berks, SL1 1DY.